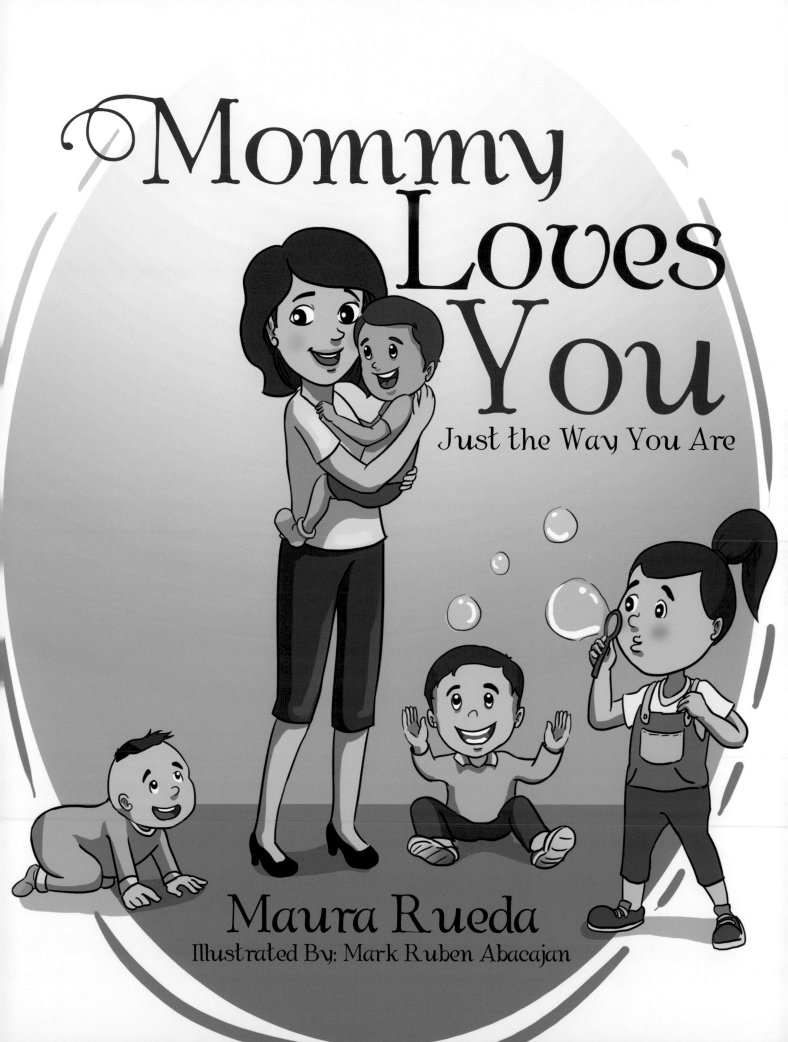

Mommy Loves You

Just the Way You Are

Maura Rueda

Illustrated By: Mark Ruben Abacajan

Print information available on the last page

Rev. date: 06/02/2016

To order additional copies of this book, contact:
Xlibris
1-888-795-4274
www.Xlibris.com
Orders@Xlibris.com

Mommy Loves You

Just the Way You Are

Dedicated to
Daneli and
Leina Rueda
With love Mom

Maura Rueda

Illustrated By: Mark Ruben Abacajan

Mommy
loves you!

Mommy loves the way you are!

Mommy loves the way you smile.

**Mommy loves the
way you laugh.**

Mommy
even loves
the way
you cry.

Mommy loves you!

Mommy loves your little eyes.

Mommy loves your little bitty feet.

Mommy even loves your dirty little hands.

Mommy loves you!

Mommy loves the way you jump.

**Mommy loves the
way you dance.**

**Mommy even loves
the way you walk.**

Mommy loves you!

Mommy loves your hugs.

Mommy loves your kisses.

Mommy loves you just the way you are!

Printed in the United States
By Bookmasters